Good King Wenceslas

verses by J. M. Neale

illustrated by JAMICHAEL HENTERLY

MACMILLAN CHILDREN'S BOOKS

0333518659

for my mother

Good King Wenceslas looked out
On the feast of Stephen

When the snow lay round about,
Deep and crisp and even.

Brightly shone the moon that night,
Though the frost was cruel,

When a poor man came in sight,
Gath'ring winter fuel.

"Hither page, and stand by me,
If thou know'st it, telling,

Yonder peasant who is he?
Where and what his dwelling?"

"Sire, he lives a good league hence,
Underneath the mountains,

Right against the forest fence
By Saint Agnes' fountain."

"Bring me food and bring me wine,
Bring me pine logs hither.

Thou and I will see him dine
When we bear them thither."

Page and monarch, forth they went,
Forth they went together,

Through the rude winds' wild lament
And the bitter weather.

"Sire, the night is darker now,
And the wind blows stronger.

Fails my heart, I know not how;
I can go no longer."

"Mark my footsteps, my good page,
Tread thou in them boldly;

Thou shalt find the winter's rage
Freeze thy blood less coldly."

In his master's steps he trod,
Where the snow lay dinted.

Heat was in the very sod
Which the saint had printed.

Therefore, gentle folk, be sure,
Wealth or rank possessing,

Ye who now will bless the poor
Shall yourselves find blessing.

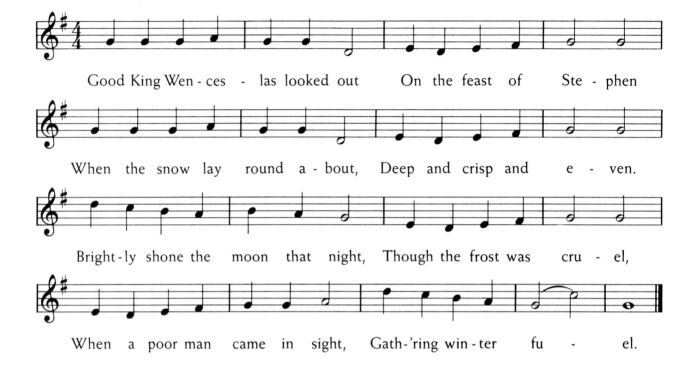

Good King Wen - ces - las looked out On the feast of Ste - phen
When the snow lay round a - bout, Deep and crisp and e - ven.
Bright - ly shone the moon that night, Though the frost was cru - el,
When a poor man came in sight, Gath - 'ring win - ter fu - el.

"Hither page, and stand by me,
  If thou know'st it, telling,
  Yonder peasant who is he?
  Where and what his dwelling?"
"Sire, he lives a good league hence,
  Underneath the mountains,
  Right against the forest fence
  By Saint Agnes' fountain."

"Bring me food and bring me wine,
  Bring me pine logs hither.
  Thou and I will see him dine
  When we bear them thither."
Page and monarch, forth they went,
  Forth they went together,
  Through the rude winds' wild lament
  And the bitter weather.

"Sire, the night is darker now,
  And the wind blows stronger.
  Fails my heart, I know not how;
  I can go no longer."
"Mark my footsteps, my good page,
  Tread thou in them boldly;
  Thou shalt find the winter's rage
  Freeze thy blood less coldly."

In his master's steps he trod,
  Where the snow lay dinted.
  Heat was in the very sod
  Which the saint had printed.
Therefore, gentle folk, be sure,
  Wealth or rank possessing,
  Ye who now will bless the poor
  Shall yourselves find blessing.